Calm, Happy Kids

23 Mindful Activities to Help Children Feel Calm, Focused and Happy

For children aged 3 to 7 and beyond

Rob Plevin

Illustrated By Kseniia Panchenko

Life Raft Media

DISCLAIMER AND/OR LEGAL NOTICES:
The information presented herein represents the view of the author as of the date of publication. This publication is for information purposes only. It is not intended to provide exact or precise advice. As such, you should use the information at your own risk.

Print ISBN: 978-1-913514-31-0
Kindle ISBN: 978-1-913514-32-7
ebook/other ISBN: 978-1-913514-33-4

Yours FREE:
167 Fun Children's Activities

As a thank you for buying this book we'd like to give you a free collection of children's activities including Arts and Crafts – Indoor Games – Outdoor Activities – Projects – Kitchen Activities – Rainy Day Fun & much more!

To get your Free Children's Activity Pack go here:
www.liferaftmedia.com/167fun

For Poppy.

Whenever I want to feel happy, I think of you.

Contents

Foreword

When Rob reached out to me about writing the foreword for Calm, Happy Kids, I told him I didn't think I was the right person. I don't have any children, and I'm pretty sure the last thing parents and caregivers want is some childless guy telling them what they need to do for their kiddos. Having fifteen nieces and nephews whom I see a handful of times a year does not an expert make me.

Then I read the book. And did the exercises. And soon realized the 23 Mindful Activities to Help Children Feel Calm, Focused and Happy actually helped me feel more calm, focused and happy. The great secret of this book is that it's not just for kids, though it will no doubt do wonders for their sense of peace, concentration and joy. This lovingly written and gorgeously illustrated guide works for parents and caregivers too, and I don't need to be a parent to know that raising children can feel, at times, like taking the fast path to insanity.

I write and speak a lot about the power of love, and self-love specifically. The relationship we build with ourselves influences every thought, word and action we take. When that relationship is centered in love, there are no limits to what we can create in our lives. This beautiful book is an invitation for kids to love themselves in a more clear and conscious way, and to have a ton of fun while doing so. It is also an invitation for parents and caregivers to love themselves, to model for their children what it looks like to be intentional about creating more calm, focus and happiness in their lives.

After all, children need to experience more than just adults who love them. They need adults who love themselves, too. Take it from this childless guy, Calm, Happy Kids will guide you and your child together into a more peaceful, joyful and love-filled reality.

Scott Stabile, Author of Big Love: The Power of Living with a Wide-Open Heart

Introduction

This book is a guide for parents, carers and children to use together. It will help children learn to manage their emotions, enabling them to feel calmer and happier.

If you're a carer or parent, it's likely you'll recognise this scene: you turn to your child in a moment of stress, and you beg, shout, or scold, "Sit still!" or "Go to sleep!" or "Calm down!" or "Concentrate!" But no matter how many times you try, it just doesn't work.

The whole situation is exhausting. Nothing takes the wind out of our sails more than knowing that our efforts will be fruitless, or worse, counterproductive. Our children often do the very opposite of what we ask, becoming even more excited, fidgety, angry or distracted. So why do we fall back on the same script, time and time again?

It's a very hard habit to break, one learned when we were children ourselves, when our parents and teachers probably said much the same things. Change is difficult, even when we know what we're doing doesn't work. This book is here to help.

The games and exercises in these pages are divided into four sections: Feeling Calm, Feeling Focused, Feeling Sleepy and Feeling Happy. They will act as a guide to help children learn to move away from states of mind and body that hold back their happiness, their chances of succeeding in hobbies they love, their school performance, and their ability to build strong, fulfilling relationships with you and other people. They will also help improve their sleep.

For children, emotions are complex. When they are told 'calm down', or 'concentrate', they may understand what is being asked, but they don't always know how to comply. Children don't always understand the steps they need to go through to make their body and mind do what you, or a teacher, or even they themselves would like. This is not unique to children. Many adults are not very good at self-regulating either, but in children the emotions are rarely masked. A child's anger, over-excitement and anxieties are often more observable.

This book teaches children, in ways they understand, how to self-regulate their emotions. With the ideas shared in the four sections, your child will begin to understand how to calm down, how to focus, how to prepare their mind and body for sleep, and how to feel happier. These are incredibly valuable life skills.

The world we live in is filled with challenges for today's children. Some have really struggled to cope with changes in routine during the global pandemic of 2020-2022. Many are affected by the profusion of screen-based information and ways of interacting with peers, and most children are also growing up in busy, working households, sometimes with little support from extended family or the wider community.

The techniques in this book will equip children with the tools they need to build a peaceful, focused, loving, adaptable, and resilient state of mind: exactly what they need in our fast-changing world.

Next time you need your child to concentrate, sit still, get a good night's rest, resist snacking and wait for dinner, or feel in control of their nerves before a test, try holding back the urge to say 'go to sleep' or 'calm down'. Instead, get them to try one of the exercises in this book. It will no longer feel like you're asking the impossible.

Practice Hints

Many activities in this collection are based on diverse mindfulness practices from all over the world. They have been selected and adapted to make them suitable for children. For example, 'Sending Happiness' in the 'Feeling Happy' section, is inspired by an ancient Buddhist practice called 'Metta'. This is a Pali word meaning 'loving-kindness and goodwill'. 'Bee Breath' in the 'Feeling Calm' section, is based on the Yogic breathing practice of 'Bhramari Pranayama'. This is often translated into 'humming bee breath' in English. In the 'Feeling Happy' section, 'Happy Heart' is inspired by HeartMath, a mind-body wellbeing approach that works with the heartbeat, and its impact on our emotional state.

The exercises are suitable for ages 3-7 and beyond. Older children may be able to read through and understand the exercises and activities with little assistance. With a younger child, you should be ready to help them, at least to begin with, reading each exercise several times as they go through the movements.

You don't have to do all the exercises regularly. You can just pick a few of your favourites and do them for a few minutes each day but it's best if the initial learning of the techniques is done when they are calm, rather than waiting until they are wound up to practice.

Once a child is skilled in these mindfulness activities, he or she can use them throughout life. Adults can also use them. In fact, it will hugely encourage your child if you learn these exercises together. The rewards of practising mindfulness, just for a short while each day, are great for you as well as your child.

A recent study* compared children who were doing a mindfulness module at school as part of a wellbeing project, with a second group of children. The second group were doing the same project, but they did not participate in the mindfulness module. Over time, the group practising mindfulness showed greater improvement in their emotional control and stress levels. They also had greater levels of empathy and optimism, and decreased depression. Their peers rated them as more sociable, less aggressive, and more popular. This finding is further supported by scientific studies, which have shown that mindfulness practices, including gratitude and meditation, increase our levels of dopamine, endorphins, serotonin and oxytocin. These are chemicals known to improve our mood and motivation, reduce aggression, insomnia and anxiety, and boost our physical health.**

It is my sincere wish that you and your children enjoy the exercises in this book. Supporting your child to learn mindfulness techniques like these has the potential to create better relationships with family and friends, more happiness, better memories, less arguing, and a mind that is ready to learn. Give them a go and see what happens.

I'd love to hear how you get on, so please get in touch and let me know. You can find me at theliferaft.org.

*

Schonert-Reichl KA, Oberle E, Lawlor MS, Abbott D, Thomson K, Oberlander TF, Diamond A. Enhancing cognitive and social-emotional development through a simple-to-administer mindfulness-based school program for elementary school children: a randomized controlled trial In. Developmental Psychology 2015 Jan;51(1):52-66.

**

For more on chemicals, mood and health see:
Ghosh Kumar, Happy Hormones at Work: Applying the learnings from Neuroscience to Improve and Sustain Workplace Happiness
Bromberg Martin et Al, Dopamine in Motivational Control: Rewarding, Aversive and Alerting.
Salamone J, The Mysterious Motivational Functions of Dopamine.
Kjaer et Al, Increased dopamine tone during meditation-induced change of consciousness.

Rokade B, Release of Endorphin Hormone and Its Effects on Our Body and Moods: A Review.

Feeling Calm

In this section, you're going to learn some techniques for feeling calm and settled. This is not always easy, especially when the feelings we have are very strong. But if you can recognise when you're angry or upset, and make yourself feel happier, or stay calm when you're worried or fidgety, you'll be able to deal with things when they get difficult. Feeling calm and changing your feelings whenever you want, even if the unexpected happens, is a bit like a superpower.

It's a good idea to practise these exercises even when you're feeling good, so that you feel ready to do them when you really need them.

Slow Walking

Sometimes the world around us is very exciting, but other times it feels too busy! We are surrounded by so many things in the world as we zoom about. It can feel good to slow down. Let's try it and see what happens.

Let your arms rest at your sides, stand tall, and take 3 long, slow, peaceful breaths.

When you're ready, try to keep breathing peacefully, and start walking very slowly. Take a few steps in super slow-motion. Try to feel your muscles working as you lift each leg. Can you feel the ground under your feet? Maybe you can even feel the fabric inside your shoes.

As you walk, what are your arms doing? Are they loosely dangling at your sides or swinging gently? Does your leg that steps forward feel different to the leg it leaves behind? Pay attention to your whole body as you keep slowly walking.

Take 10 slow, careful steps.

Now just stand still for a little while. Take a long slow breath in, and hold it for a couple of seconds. Then breathe all the way out.

Did going in slow-motion make you feel relaxed?

Scented Candle

Smells can be very calming. What is your favourite? You could choose something tasty, like freshly baked bread, or hot chocolate, or you could pick a smell from outside, like the grass, or the sea.

Make sure you're sitting comfortably, then close your eyes and imagine a scented candle that burns with your favourite smell.

Take a deep breath in and let the lovely smell fill your whole body. Imagine it filling you up, in through your nose and all the way down to your toes. Let it warm and relax you. Mmmmm, lovely.

Now slowly breathe out.

Let's do it again: take a long, slow breath in and imagine your favourite smell is filling your body. Try to feel it in your fingertips. Let it tingle all the way down your body to your toes.

Now take a long slow breath out, all the way.

Great job! Slowly open your eyes.
Remember to think of your favourite smell whenever you want to feel calm.

Bee Breath

This is a very special breathing technique to help quiet your thoughts and calm your mind. It's perfect for when your mind is chattering away and making you restless.

On a warm summer's day, when the flowers are in bloom, have you noticed the bumble bees? They buzz around contentedly with sticky little legs, and big fat tummies full with all the delicious flowers they have sipped from. They sound like they are humming away happily to themselves, don't they? That's the noise you're going to make.

Take a deep breath in through your nose.

Breathe out, very slowly, but keep your mouth closed.

Make a humming sound and keep humming until you need to breathe in again.

Did you sound just like a bumble bee? Let's try it again. Ready? Slowly breathe all the way in through your nose.

As you slowly breathe out, make your humming noise with

your mouth closed. Imagine you're one of those friendly, fuzzy bees, bumbling from flower to flower, getting more and more peaceful with each breath.

Hmmmmmmmmm.

Five Things

Whenever you feel on edge, you can use this trick to calm yourself down. It's a little bit like the game 'I Spy', but you don't need anyone else to play.

Start by taking three slow, deep breaths in and out through your nose.

Now look around you. Can you spy five things around you? In your head, say the name of each thing you choose.

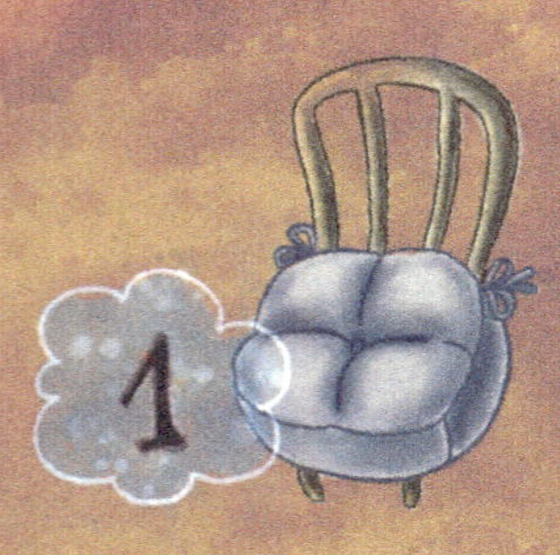

The next step is to do the same thing again, but this time you've got to spy a bit deeper. This time you're going to keep your eyes closed and name five things you can feel. Can you feel the floor under your feet? Maybe the cushion you're sitting on? The fabric of your clothes?

Your ears would like to go next – this time you're going to pick five things you can hear. What sounds are around you? Listen for five things. Is there a radio playing, traffic passing, a phone ringing, maybe a bird singing?

Well done. You're a good listener.

Let's do this four more times. Each time you spy, or feel, or hear the things around you, you can look for one less thing, and it's fine to repeat things.

Is your mind more settled now?

3 Steps to Feeling Calm

Imagine what it would be like if you had a tool in your pocket that could make you feel calm whenever you wanted. That's exactly what this exercise is and it takes just 3 simple steps!

Step #1: Stop whatever you're doing to focus on your feet. How do they feel? Notice if they are cold or warm, if they are curled up or relaxed. Maybe you can feel a wrinkle in your sock, or a stone under the sole of your shoe.

Step #2: Bring your attention to your hands.
Just lay them flat on the table or on your knees, and let them be still for a few moments. How do your hands feel?

Step #3: Think about your breathing.
Keeping your feet and hands still, see if you can follow a very slow, deep breath from start to finish. Feel it going all the way into your body, from your nose, right into your chest, and down into your tummy.

After a short pause, feel it rising up again, flowing into your chest, and out of your nose. Try breathing in the same way two more times. Feel the slow, deep breaths all the way in... and all the way out.

Just breathe normally now, and see how you feel. Do you feel calmer?

Nostrils Taking Turns

This is a fun way to breathe that helps you feel calm. You can do it anywhere, and any time, almost... maybe you'd best to not do this at a posh dinner party. Although, if you did, you could say, "Excuse me, ladies and gentlemen, I'm just practising my 'nadi shodhan pranayama'". That would be impressive! Those big words are the fancy name for a Yogic breath control practice, and that's what this exercise is based on.

We're going to breathe in a special pattern so that air goes in through one nostril, and out through the other. It's a bit like a train going through a tunnel. Ready?

Use your right thumb to gently close your right nostril. Keeping your right nostril shut, take a slow breath in through your left nostril.

Once the train of air has flowed in, let go with your thumb and use your finger to close your left nostril. Slowly let the air out of your right nostril.

Now the train changes direction. Keeping your left nostril closed with your finger, slowly breathe in again through your right nostril. Now, let go of the left nostril and close your right nostril with your thumb again. Slowly, breathe out through your left nostril.

Try and repeat this pattern a few times. It gets easier with practice. Just try to take it nice and slow. If you get muddled, don't worry, just try again. Keep practising, building up to two or three minutes of breathing with your nostrils taking turns.

Feeling Focused

Are you what someone might call a 'fidget'? Are you a wriggly jiggly, never-sit-still-for-five-minutes, ants-in-the-pants kind of person? Do you get distracted and find it hard not to move very quickly from one game or activity to another? If that sounds like you, then you're in the right place.

First of all, don't worry. You're not alone. Lots of people find it very hard to make their busy brains stay focused.

Your brain is actually one of the most powerful, incredible machines in the world. And once you learn to use more of that brain power, by learning to be more focused, pretty soon you'll be amazing at learning things.

It could be something physical, like perfecting your front crawl in the pool, or something you do at school, like learning fractions, or learning to play a musical instrument, or learning your lines for a school play.

When you learn to focus like a laser, you can do anything you put your mind to and that's what this section is all about.

How Much Can You Remember?

This is an easy and fun game you can play with a friend or a grown-up. It's based on 'Kim's Game' which was a game first mentioned in a Rudyard Kipling book over 120

years ago. It's a fun way to train your brain to focus and concentrate.

All you need for this are ten to fifteen small objects. Put all the objects together on the floor or a table.

Show the other person all the objects. Let them look at everything for a little before closing their eyes or turning away while you take away one of the items. Now the other person can look at all the items and they have to try and remember which one is missing.

Take turns to be the person who takes away the objects, or to be the person who tries to remember them, because it's fun both ways.

Now it's your turn. How many will you remember?

Flamingo Foot

Can you rub your tummy and pat your head at the same time? It's tricky, right? This exercise is really good for your brain because it gives you practice at doing two things at the same time – improving your focus and your balance.

First, pick a spot. It could be a cross on the floor, or a photograph on the wall. Whatever it is, you've got to keep your eyes pinned on it all the time!

Now you're going to stand like a flamingo. Did you know, flamingos can stand on one leg while they look for food? They can even reach down and catch a fish, all while standing on one leg. They have great focus, and great balance.

Don't worry, you don't have to catch a fish. You just have to do these two simple things at the same time... stand on one leg, and keep your eyes pinned to the spot you chose.

Are you still there? If you are, you're doing very well!

How long can you stand like a flamingo? How still can you be? Once you've stood as long as you can on one leg, see if your other leg can do even better.

Arrive and Five

When you arrive somewhere, the park, or the beach, or a waiting room, or you get on a bus, or a train, take a minute to try this activity. It's a handy, on-the-go version of the 'Five Things' activity in the 'Feeling Calm' section, and it's a great way to train yourself to notice your surroundings and focus your mind.

All you've got to do when you arrive somewhere new is look around and pick any five things you can see. So, if you were on a beach, you might say: "seagull, boat, sandcastle, towel, shell".

Next, all you've got to do is close your eyes, and try to remember those five things. To make it more interesting, see if you can use whole sentences to describe each thing you choose:

The noisy seagull with the speckled feathers.

The pretty boat with the white sails.

The sandcastle that's just about to wash away.

The towel with the yellow stripes.

The shell with a tiny hole.

You could also make up new rules. Maybe you're only allowed to look for blue things. Or perhaps you've got to find five things that start with any of the letters in your name.

How about saying the words "arrive and five!" whenever you arrive somewhere new. It will be a reminder to look at the world around you.

The Sit Still Challenge

Have you ever played musical statues at a party? When the music stops, you've got to stand really still, not moving at all. It's quite hard, isn't it? But did you know this is a skill you can practise?

You can get better at keeping still, even if you're a person who really loves to move about, even if you're a person who is always told to "stop being fidgety", even if you find being still impossible! With practise, absolutely everyone can get better at keeping still.

We're going to do this exercise sitting on a chair, so you should find a nice comfy seat. You'll also need a grown-up with a timer and a few minutes to watch you carefully, just like a musical chairs judge.

Start the timer and keep really still. Imagine you're glued to your chair. If your hands are resting on your knees, use your imagination to glue them down. Use the imaginary glue to stick the soles of your shoes to the floor. This means you can't scratch your nose, and you can't swing your feet forwards and backwards. You can't even whisper! You're allowed to breathe gently though, and if you prefer to keep your eyes open, you're allowed to blink.

Try this a couple of times a week, and write down how long you can sit before you move. This activity is training you to control your body, and over time you'll find out that you get better and better at it.

Balancing Rocks

Building towers out of rocks is a game that will boost your concentration and your focus. This is a tricky activity but if you stick at it, it will help you learn to be patient and to deal with challenges. These are both great skills to have.

First, you'll need to find some nice, flat, solid ground to be your foundation. Then you'll need a good, flat rock to form the base of your tower. Can you find another rock that sits firmly on top? See how many more you can add to the tower. You'll need to pay attention and look carefully at the different shapes and angles in each rock to try and fit them together and not knock the whole thing down. And you'll need patience to keep trying again and again if the rocks fall down. Oh, and don't forget to breathe nice and slowly as you do this. When we're concentrating, it's very easy to forget!

Try this game whenever there are rocks around, in the garden, at a beach or by a river. Each time you play the game you'll be improving your focus and your ability to keep going and overcome challenges.

Chew Slowly Like a Cow

Eating slowly can be a challenge, but learning not to rush is very good for you. It helps you enjoy your meals even more, helps your body digest your food and it helps you learn to be calm and to take your time. For this activity you'll need something small to eat. A raisin would be ideal.

Start by picking up your chosen snack and having a good, long look at it. How does it look? Is it shiny, or plump, or wrinkly?

How does it feel when you touch it? Is it smooth, or rough, or moist, or dry, hard or soft?

How would you describe the smell? Does the smell remind you of anything? Does it make you remember someone, or a place? Perhaps you remember being at the sea, being at nursery school, or visiting a friend's house. You might think about a celebration when this food was on the table. Now it's finally time to put the snack to your lips. Roll it slowly onto your tongue and hold it in your mouth without chewing it. Can you taste anything yet? How does it feel?

What does it feel like as you begin to chew? What does it taste like? Do you think you can chew slowly, like a cow, without swallowing it straight away?

When you're ready, you can swallow your snack. Did it feel different when you ate slowly and concentrated on your food?

Feeling Happy

Sometimes, things happen that we can't control, and these things can make us feel sad. Sometimes, we just feel a bit fed up. Knowing how to make yourself feel more positive is a great skill to learn, and this can really help you cope if difficult things do happen.

This section is all about helping you feel happier. It's about finding joy in the small things all around you, and learning how good it is to share that joy. The best bit is you can experience this whenever you want... every single day, starting right now. Let's get to it!

The Gratitude Tree

Scientists have discovered that when we feel thankful or grateful, it brings all kinds of benefits, including making us happier and more cheerful! In this activity, you're going to decorate a beautiful, imaginary tree with all the good things you've got in your life. You can picture this tree whenever you want to cheer yourself up.

Close your eyes and take three slow, deep belly breaths. Try to imagine a special tree in your mind. It can be a real tree you like visiting, or even one you've climbed. It could be a tree from a book you've read, or one you've made up. It's your special tree.

As you picture your tree, think about something you feel grateful for. Maybe you feel thankful that something wonderful has happened to you recently. Perhaps you've got a special skill or talent that means a lot to you. You could feel grateful for a special toy, a good friend, or a kind teacher. Maybe you're grateful for good weather at the weekend, or for someone in your family, or for a pet who keeps you company.

Picture each thing you're grateful for, one thing at a time. You can imagine a photograph of each thing and tie the photograph up in the tree with some coloured ribbon.

Whenever you want to feel happier, you can think of your tree to remind yourself of all the wonderful things in your life.

The Magic Balloons

Magic Balloons carry away uncomfortable feelings. You know those grouchy, angry feelings that seem to tie you up in knots? Here's a little secret: you can just let these feelings go whenever you choose to, and then you can feel calmer and happier. Here's how...

Close your eyes and imagine three big grey balloons bobbing above you on strings.

Grey balloons are full of sad, unhappy and angry feelings. Look up and pick a balloon you don't like. Feel the end of the string in your hand. You know what to do now! Let go of the string and watch one of the grey balloons float up and away, taking all those uncomfortable feelings with it.

Now you've made room for a new balloon. This one is bright yellow. It is full of happy, good things. Maybe a funny memory or someone who loves you. Can you see a big yellow balloon in the bunch?

Shall we let another grey one go?

Up... up... up and away. Off go the yucky feelings.
Now you've got room for another yellow balloon. Listen to this one carefully, and you might hear a giggle inside. Your yellow balloons are filled with joy.

There's one grey balloon left to send on its way. Let it take all the sad, unhappy feelings with it. Watch it disappear.

Now you've got three yellow balloons, each one filled with happy thoughts and feelings. Do you feel better?

Your Happy Journal

Keeping a happy journal is an easy, fun way to boost your happiness each day, and it only takes a few minutes. Just before you go to bed is a great time to fill your journal in, and this might quickly become one of your favourite activities, a daily habit for years to come!

You can make your own happy journal by decorating a notebook with stickers, pens or glitter. You could cover it with pictures or photographs. Try to make it as special as you can.

What should you write about? Your journal is a place to write down anything that helps you feel good. Think about what was good about your day, any challenges you've overcome, and all the things you're thankful for.

You could also write about the positive feelings you've had. What made you excited? What made you feel happy? What have you worked hard at or overcome? What did you get better at?

This is also a good time to think about the other people who were part of your day. What did you do today that made someone smile? What did someone else do that made you feel happy today?

Your journal is a place to write down or draw anything that helps you feel good: a list of your favourite books or places to visit, drawings of your favourite sports or activities or simply a positive motto or mantra.

You could finish your journal entry with a little drawing of a face with an expression to show how you feel overall about your day.

Sending Happiness

Did you know you can experience lovely warm feelings of happiness simply by thinking kind thoughts towards other people? You can try this any time, but it's particularly nice to do it at the end of the day, before you go to sleep.

Take a deep breath. Hold it for a few seconds and slowly let it go.

Now, can you think now about a person, or a thing, that makes you feel full up to the brim with happiness?

Can you feel that happiness in your chest or tummy, glowing like a warm sun?

Feel that happy warm feeling overflowing and spreading like syrup or melted chocolate through your whole body.

Who would you like to share some happiness with? Picture them in front of you, and as you send them some of these happy feelings, see them smiling. You can smile back at them, if you like. When you do, you send them even more happiness. Do you see how their smile gets bigger and bigger? Does it make you feel happier too?

Happiness is a really good feeling to share. You can try it with more people that you love and care for, or even a pet.

You could try sending happiness to someone you think might be feeling sad or lonely.

How do you feel when you make others smile?

Body Smile

Smiling and laughing feels good, doesn't it? In this exercise you're going to spread a wonderful feeling of happiness all over your body simply by thinking about smiling.

Close your eyes and take 3 deep, slow belly breaths.

In...

Out...

Once your body is peaceful, try to picture someone that makes you smile. It can be anyone at all, as long as you feel a lovely, happy feeling in your tummy when you think of them.

Imagine yourself smiling at them. You could even try curling your lips up, actually smiling as you think of them. Can you see them smiling back at you? What does it feel like when you imagine smiling at each other? It's nice, isn't it?

Now, let us take this nice, smiley, happy feeling and send

it round your body to all those parts that get forgotten about.

Smile at your chest. Can you feel your chest and tummy enjoying being smiled at?

Smile at your back from the top to the bottom. Can you feel your back feeling happier?

Smile at your arms and shoulders.

Smile at your legs and feet.

Smile at your whole body, and feel your whole body smiling from the inside out.

Full of happiness.

Full of smiles.

Happy Heart

The rhythm of your heartbeat can change depending on your mood and your feelings. If your heart beats with a steady, even rhythm, you will find it easier to concentrate, and you'll feel happy and calm. This exercise makes you more aware of the beating of your heart, and the more time you spend on it, the better you'll get at staying happy and calm.

Place your hands on your chest and feel your hands

warming your heart. Focus on your heart as you breathe the warmth slowly in and out.

Each time you breathe in, imagine you're breathing in through your heart. Each time you breathe out, imagine you're breathing out through your heart. Try doing 10 breaths like this.

Well done. Now think of someone or something that makes you feel really, really happy.

It could be anything, your favourite place to go, or a game, or a special person. Does the thought of this thing make you feel happiness? Can you feel yourself starting to smile?

Let that happy feeling grow in your heart, as if your heart is also smiling. If you pay close attention, it will feel good in your whole chest, as if your heart is glowing with happiness.

Once you've got that feeling of love and happiness shining in you, why not try sending it out to your family and friends? You can send the feeling to anyone you like. Picture them in your mind, picture them, and send them the lovely warm, smiley feelings. Does it feel nice?

Feeling Sleepy

Do you sleep like a log? Or do you find yourself thrashing like a crocodile under your duvet, and throwing your pillow across the room? Not being able to get to sleep is really annoying, isn't it? Feeling uncomfortable, getting tangled up in your sheets, staring at the ceiling. It's a horrible feeling.

If this happens to you, don't worry. It happens to lots of children and adults as well. In this section you'll find some activities you can do that will make falling asleep much easier.

Gather the Light

This activity takes away all your restless energy, and makes you feel calm and sleepy at bed time.

Stand with your feet slightly apart and your arms by your sides.

Close your eyes.

Slowly raise your arms out to the side with your palms facing up. As you do, imagine that you're going to gather all the beautiful, glowing light from the moon, and bring it down through your body. This light is very calming for your mind and your body.

Gather all the light by moving your arms slowly up over your head until your hands are facing each other.

Well done. Now, all the moonlight is between your hands like a big glowing ball. Put your palms down on top of the ball and slowly push the light down through your head, your neck, your chest, your tummy, your hips, and your legs.

As the light passes through you it takes away all the fluttering, fidgety feelings that keep you awake. The wonderful calming moonlight is washing away all your twitchy feelings, sending them down through your legs and feet, away into the ground.

Let's try it again. Ready?

Each time you gather the moonlight and push it down over your body, it gathers up more and more fidgety feelings, and washes them through your feet, down into the ground.

Try doing this super-slowly 10 times to feel ready for a peaceful, dreamy sleep.

Squish

In this exercise, you'll make your muscles relax one by one by tightening or squishing them, and then letting them go.

Lie down flat on your back with your legs straight and your arms down by your sides. You can do this in bed if you like.

Start by giving your head, face and neck a really good squish. Close your eyes tight, rumple your nose and screw up your face as if you've just tasted something nasty. Squish your face as tight as you can for the count of five... 5, 4, 3, 2, 1. And relax. Wonderful!

Now, it's time for your hands, arms and shoulders. Squeeze your fists, and feel all the muscles in your arms and shoulders working hard. Ready to hold for five? SQUISH!

5, 4, 3, 2, 1. Great work.

Next your chest, tummy and back. Give them a really good squish and hold for the count of five. Ready?

5, 4, 3, 2, 1. And let go. Well done!

Okay, let's move down to your bottom, your legs and your feet. Squish your leg muscles and your bottom as tight as you can. Curl your toes down really tightly. Make the muscles feel hard and strong and give everything a really good, long squish. Here goes:

5, 4, 3, 2, 1. Now, relax.

Let's do one more super-huge squish. This time you're going to tighten your whole body. Ready? SQUISH!

5, 4, 3, 2, 1. Brilliant.

Now you can let go and breathe deeply. Are you feeling really floppy, relaxed and calm?

Belly Breathing

This is a breathing technique that will help you feel calm at bedtime. It encourages your body and mind to relax so you can fall asleep easier.

It's best to learn this technique lying down, but once you've mastered it you can practise it sitting or even standing too. To help you learn, find something to balance on your tummy, like a small stuffed toy.

Lie down somewhere comfortable and put the toy on top of your belly button. Once your toy is balanced, let your arms drop to your sides with your palms facing up. Now breathe in through your nose very slowly.

Feel your tummy fill with air like a big balloon. Be slow and gentle so your stuffed animal doesn't lose its balance. If it does fall off, that's fine, just pop it back in position. As you're breathing these deep belly breaths, you should see the stuffed toy going up and down.

Breathe out slowly, and as you feel your belly going down, pull your belly button in towards your back. This movement really helps squeeze out all the air – just like squeezing all the toothpaste out of a tube.

As you breathe in again, imagine you are filling up the balloon in your belly. Then slowly squeeze the toothpaste out of the tube on the out-breath.

Keep practising, and remember to keep this movement steady and slow. How long can you keep your stuffed toy balanced on your belly?

Square Breathing

Once you've mastered the Belly Breathing exercise you can build on it using this technique. This exercise is used by people in emergency services to help them cope with stressful situations. It makes your body and mind feel very relaxed making it perfect for bedtime.

You can do this lying down or sitting in a comfy chair. A cushion isn't essential but you can use one to help you keep count when you first start out.

Tap your hand along one edge of the cushion as you start to breathe in very slowly. Breathe in slowly enough to count all the way to four in your head, and tap each count as you go... 1, 2, 3, 4. Remember to take it slow!

Once you've taken your full four beat breath, hold your breath for another count of four. As you hold your breath, you can tap out a count of four on the next edge of the cushion.... 1, 2, 3, 4.

Now you're ready to breathe out. Tap your hand on another edge of the cushion as you slowly breathe out... 1, 2, 3, 4.

Now you're going to hold your breath once again for another count of four. As you hold your breath, you can tap out a count of four on the last edge of the cushion: 1, 2, 3, 4.

Let's go through another cycle together:

Breathe in for four beats: 1, 2, 3, 4.

Hold your breath for four beats: 1, 2, 3, 4.

Breathe out for four beats: 1, 2, 3, 4.

And hold your breath for four beats: 1, 2, 3, 4.

Try this cycle another 4 times and notice how calm it makes you feel.

Shake Off Your Fidgets

Shaking is a GREAT way to calm your body. Just as dogs shake water off their fur, you can shake off all those fidgety annoying feelings that stop you from feeling calm and sleepy.

Start by standing with your feet slightly apart. Now, take three slow deep breaths and hold the third one.

Get ready to breathe out and shake off your fidgets at the same time. Ready?

Breathe out and shake your arms all the way from your shoulders to your fingers. Let all those fidgets go flying away like droplets of water.

Shake them up in the air and down to the ground.

Shake your legs as if you've got paws covered in mud. Shake your body like a crazy puppy with a shaggy coat.

Shake, shake, shake. Get rid of all those fidgets.

Shall we do it again once more? Take 3 breaths and hold the last one. Ready to shake?

GO!

Breathe out and shake off your fidgets.

Once you've had a really good shake, you can lie on the floor or sit on a comfy chair and take another long, deep breath. And as you slowly breathe out, let any final fidgets gently evaporate, leaving you feeling lovely and calm.

Sunny Snooze

When we find it difficult to sleep, it can be because we feel discomfort or jumpiness in our bodies. This activity helps you relax by concentrating on different parts of your body, one part at a time. You can practise it during the day to help your body feel more relaxed, or at night before you go to sleep.

Find a comfy place to lie down. Close your eyes and take three long, slow, deep breaths. Good.

Now imagine the sun is shining down on you, warming your whole body. Feel it shining on the top of your head and notice how your head feels in the warm sun.

Take another deep breath. Imagine the warm sunbeams touching your forehead and slipping down over your whole face. The warm sun on your cheeks makes you smile.

You can make the sun move over you at whatever pace you enjoy. There is no rush. This is a long snoozy summer's day. When you're ready, let the sun start to move down your neck, over your shoulders, past your elbows, and all the way to your fingertips. Let the sunshine slip over your hands, feeling the warmth around each finger.

Feel the sunshine on your chest, and your back. If you find yourself moving, that's okay, just bring your thoughts back to the warm sun on your body.

Now feel your tummy warmed by the sun. Feel it shining on your hips, and your thighs. Feel it moving down over your knees, down even more, over your lower legs, your feet and your toes.

Soon the sun will start to move down your body again. Try it one more time from the top of your head, moving slowly down, warming and relaxing each part of your body. Enjoy the feeling of it moving down your chest, along your arms, and reaching each fingertip again. It moves over your hips, under your thighs, over your knees, and gently on to your feet and toes.

Now your whole body is warm and calm. You can lie here in the sun for as long as you want.

Resources

Books

Books by Poppy O'Neill

Poppy O'Neill is an author specialising in children's mental and emotional health. 'Don't Worry, Be Happy' and '101 Ways to Help Your Anxious Child' are both available on Amazon or on Poppy's website. You can find the full range here: **www.poppyoneill.com/shop/**

The HappySelf Journal

My 7-year-old daughter loves this award-winning journal and we've bought quite a few of them over the years. It's beautifully illustrated and very engaging with ready-made prompts and activities for expressing gratitude and reflecting on behaviours, thoughts and emotions. Thousands of parents whose children have used the HappySelf Journal have reported better sleep, reduced anxiety, improved connection and communication, increased kindness, and more positive mindsets in their children. **www.happyselfjournal.com**

Training

Parenting for Connection

Parenting expert Robbin McManne was a busy 'Angry Mom' before discovering the world of peaceful parenting. She has since dedicated her life to teaching parents how to build connection and find more joy and cooperation so their kids can thrive. Robbin's work focuses on building and strengthening the parent-child relationship so that children grow up with resilience, confidence and strong emotional intelligence. She works with parents to help them understand their own emotions and frustrations in parenting, so they can help build their children's sense of self without losing themselves in the process.
Download Robbin's Free Guide, "How to Turn a NO Into Cooperation" at **www.triggerfreeparents.com**

Connected Kids

Lorraine E Murray is founder of the Connected Kids programme. For 20+ years it has helped adults teach their kids and teens meditation. Lorraine is a published author (and foster mum) with 3 books about teaching meditation. The programme helps all children but specialises on working with kids with SEN, autism, ADHD or trauma.
www.connected-kids.com

Wellbeing for Kids

Tara Russo, who has been a teacher for over 25 years, is a mindfulness and meditation coach for children and young people. She helps them to manage and process their uncomfortable emotions, such as anger and anxiety. She empowers them by giving them mindful tools to self-regulate their behaviour and impulses. Tara's adult trainees also learn more about how to manage their own stress levels in a relaxed and friendly space. For more information, please see www.wellbeingforkidsuk.com

Youth Mindfulness

The Youth Mindfulness Kids Programme is 16 one-hour lessons, jam-packed with games, videos and activities that make mindfulness fun and inspiring for 7-11 year olds. The programme draws on the latest evidence base from the science of wellbeing, as well as decades of research into best practice of how to teach mindfulness. It's been taught to 100,000s of children in more than 35 countries and focuses on the cultivation of qualities that help any child to flourish: self-awareness, emotional intelligence, joyfulness, self-compassion, resilience, and kindness.
www.youthmindfulness.org

Podcasts, Apps & Tools

Zen Parenting Radio

The Zen Parenting Radio podcast combines self-awareness and mindfulness with pop culture and humour to expand compassion for ourselves, each other, and the world.
www.zenparentingradio.com

Circle Round

Circle Round adapts folktales from around the world into sound- and music-rich audio stories for kids and families. The stories are brought to life by beloved voices from the stage, screen, and public radio/media. Circle Round explores universal themes like friendship, persistence, creativity and generosity, and each episode ends with an activity that inspires a deeper conversation between children and grown-ups.
https://www.wbur.org/podcasts/circleround

Ahway Island

Since 2017, Be Calm on Ahway Island® Podcast has become a treasured part of bedtime and naptime routines for young children and their families worldwide. Each episode contains a kid-friendly meditation followed by an original, gentle story featuring a lovable cast of recurring characters. Every episode includes self-soothing techniques and positive learning messages, such as gratitude, patience, mindfulness, inclusivity, curiosity, and empathy. www.ahwayisland.com

The Rebel Girls App

Rebel Girls is a global empowerment brand dedicated to raising the most inspired and confident generation of girls through extraordinary real-life stories, experiences, products, and community. Unlock a universe of immersive, inspiring stories and discover the incredible accomplishments of women throughout history and around the world.
Find out more at www.rebelgirls.com

Stixmindfulness

Stixmindfulness provide screen-free electronic devices designed to introduce mindfulness to children at an early age by making it fun. The devices take your child through engaging therapeutic mindful activities involving balance, deep breathing, storytelling guided meditations and more. A companion app encourages continued practice.
www.stixmindfulness.co.uk

About Us

Rob Plevin – author

I'm a children's behaviour specialist, mindfulness trainer and parent. After a career as a special ed. schoolteacher for children with behaviour challenges, I spent 15 years training teachers to better understand and connect with young people before training to teach mindfulness in 2011. These days I spend my working hours running a small publishing company and delivering mindfulness-based courses on compassion and resilience from our digital home at www.theliferaft.org. I live in the ever-so-beautiful Eden valley with my wife, daughter and a strange little dog called Bodhi and when I'm not working I enjoy being outdoors and doing things with my family. I can often be found wild swimming in nearby lakes and tarns and I've recently discovered the joy of tennis (although I can't hit the ball straight). I love playing the drums to recordings of AC/DC.

Kseniia Panchenko – Illustrator

I have the best job in the world - illustrating books for kids! I have worked with authors from the US, Australia, Costa Rica, Germany, Netherlands and the UK.

My mother is a librarian and as a child I had access to a huge number of books. The illustrations became the most important thing for me in determining whether I liked a book or not. As a child, I loved pictures with lots of small details, those that were most interesting to look at; they fascinated me and awakened my imagination. Today, in the illustrator's shoes, I try to recreate the extraordinary world that surrounded me in my childhood.

An inexhaustible source of inspiration comes from my dog, Milosh. He's a miniature Schnauzer and even though he's fully grown, he still acts like a playful puppy. We love walking through the streets and parks together, sitting on the grass or playing in the snow. His positivity and carefree outlook on life makes me happy and reminds me not to take things too seriously.

I believe it's very important to keep at least a bit of childhood inside yourself and let it flow from time to time. There is a saying I like to keep in my mind about this: adults, don't grow up, it's a trap!

Eleanor Thom - editor

For me, writing is definitely where I find my calm, my focus, and my happy. As for sleep, if I am being honest, you are more likely to find me sat up in the small hours, typing away. I've been writing professionally for twelve years.

I live in Edinburgh and I have two children: a cartoonist and violinist aged 11, and 7 year old para swimmer with her sights on the Paralympics. One of the best and most surprising things about having children, for me, is watching their passions and interests take shape. I was appallingly bad at sport, especially swimming, so my daughter's swimming thing came out of the blue. It's 100% her, and I love that. It's where she finds her focus, and her happy.

Many of the techniques in this book struck a chord with me. Simple visualisations and games helped us get through hundreds of physiotherapy sessions, anxiety about operations, house moves, mood swings, and all the normal ups and downs of life.

Made in the USA
Monee, IL
04 May 2023